Languages of the World

Mandarin

Lucia Raatma

Heinemann Library
Chicago, Illinois

www.heinemannraintree.com
Visit our website to find out
more information about
Heinemann-Raintree books.

To order:
☎ Phone 888-454-2279
💻 Visit www.heinemannraintree.com
to browse our catalog and order online.

©2012 Heinemann Library
an imprint of Capstone Global Library, LLC
Chicago, Illinois

Edited by Dan Nunn, Rebecca Rissman, and
    Catherine Veitch
Designed by Marcus Bell
Picture research by Ruth Blair
Production by Victoria Fitzgerald
Originated by Capstone Global Library Ltd
Printed and bound in China by South China Printing
    Company Ltd

15 14 13 12 11
10 9 8 7 6 5 4 3 2 1

**Library of Congress Cataloging-in-
Publication Data**
Raatma, Lucia.
    Mandarin / Lucia Tarbox Raatma.
        p. cm.—(Languages of the world)
    Includes bibliographical references and index.
    ISBN 978-1-4329-5084-2—ISBN 978-1-4329-5091-
0 (pbk.) 1. Chinese language—Textbooks for foreign
speakers—English. 2. Chinese language—Spoken Chinese.
I. Title.
    PL1129.E25R33 2012
    495.1'82421—dc22
                                    2010043790

Acknowledgments
We would like to thank the following for permission to
reproduce photographs: Alamy pp. 9 (© travelib china),
13 (© Glow Asia RF), 15 (© Alan Howden – USA Stock
Photography); Corbis pp. 8 (© Hulton-Deutsch Collection),
19 (© Liu Liqun), 23 (© Yi Lu); Shutterstock pp. 5
(© AJP), 6 (© Elena Elisseeva), 7 (© Tan Wei Ming),
10 (© James Stuart Griffith), 11 (© Maria Weidner),
12 (© Stephen Coburn), 14 (© grafica), 16 (©
AVAVA), 17 (© tonobalaguerf), 18 (© 06photo), 20
(© Adrin Shamsudin), 21 (© Wong Sze Yuen), 22 (©
mamahoohooba), 24 (© testing), 25 (© JinYoung Lee),
26 (© Martin Turzak), 27 (© fotohunter), 29 (© EcoPrint).

Cover photograph of girl reproduced with permission of
Corbis (© David Katzenstein/Citizen Stock).

We would like to thank Rong Guo for her invaluable help
in the preparation of this book.

Contents

Mandarin words are in italics, *like this*. You can find out how to say them by looking in the pronunciation guide.

Mandarin Around the World

Mandarin is a language spoken mostly in China, Taiwan, and Singapore. China is a large country in Asia. Taiwan and Singapore are both small islands.

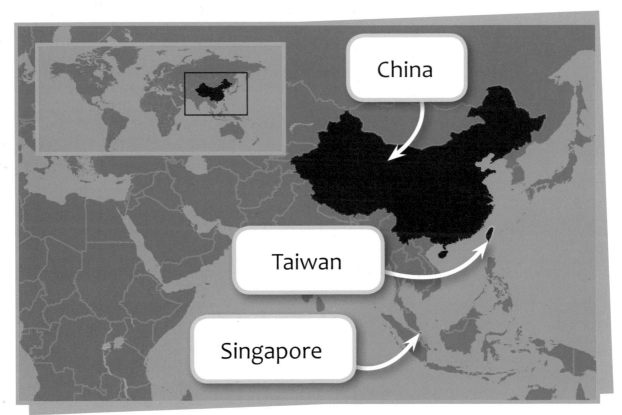

China

Taiwan

Singapore

There are Mandarin speakers in Chinatowns all over the world.

Mandarin is also spoken around the world. People have moved from China and live throughout Europe, North America, South America, and Australia. Many speak Mandarin in addition to other languages.

Who speaks Mandarin?

There are more than 1 billion Mandarin speakers around the world. In China, Mandarin is the main language. But people also use other languages, such as Tibetan, Cantonese, and Manchu.

Most people in China speak Mandarin.

Millions of people in the United States trace their backgrounds to China.

In the United States, nearly 700,000 people speak Mandarin. In the United Kingdom, about 12,000 people speak Mandarin. There are Mandarin speakers in Canada, Russia, Indonesia, and many other countries, too.

History of the Mandarin Language

For years there were many types of Chinese languages, or dialects, in China. People who lived in different parts of China spoke in different dialects. Over one hundred years ago a few government leaders began using Mandarin.

Many Chinese leaders spoke in Mandarin.

Children in Chinese schools today write and speak in Mandarin.

Mandarin became more popular. Today, Mandarin is taught in Chinese schools. Government documents are also written in Mandarin.

Learning Mandarin

The Chinese alphabet is very different from English. Pinyin is a way of using the English alphabet that shows how to say Mandarin. For example, the English letter "G" is shown as 吉 in Mandarin. In Pinyin, it is *ji*.

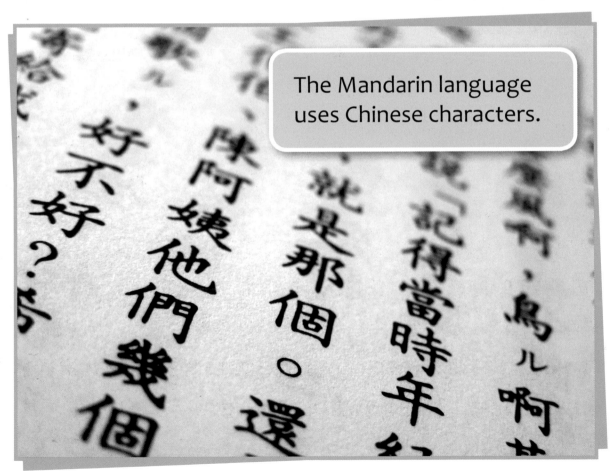

The Mandarin language uses Chinese characters.

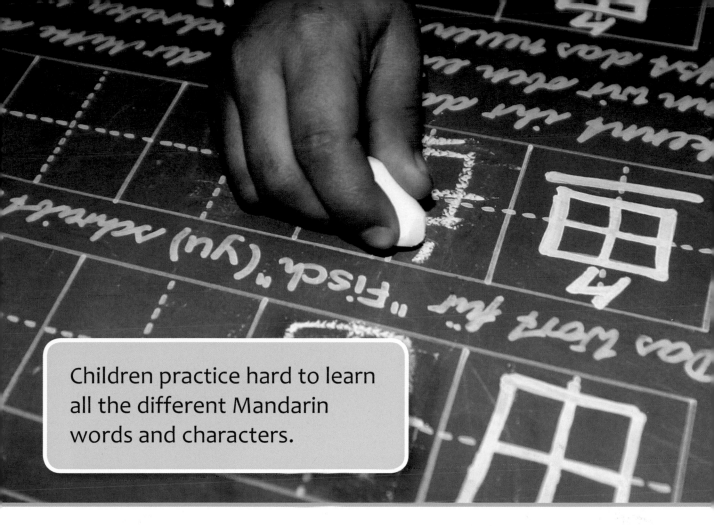

Children practice hard to learn all the different Mandarin words and characters.

Mandarin is a tonal language. That means sounds are loud and soft in different words. The tones or sounds affect what the word means. For example, *ma* can mean "mother", or "horse," depending on how it is said.

Saying Hello and Goodbye

There are many ways to greet people in China. One way is to offer a slight bow. Another way is to shake hands. Handshakes in China are usually held for longer than in other countries.

How to say it
bow = *jugong*
handshake = *woshou*
smile = *weixiao*

How to say it
Hello = *Ni hao*
Good morning = *Zaochen hao*
Goodbye = *Zaijian*

Mandarin speakers greet one another with "*Ni hao*" ("Hello") or "*Zaochen hao*" ("Good morning"). Later, they say, "*Zaijian*" ("Goodbye").

Talking About Yourself

In Mandarin the way to introduce yourself is *"Wo jiao ..."* ("My name is ..."). Then you might say, *"Hen gaoxing renshi ni"* ("Pleased to meet you").

How to say it
My name is ... = *Wo jiao ...*
Pleased to meet you =
     Hen gaoxing renshi ni

How to say it
I am from ... = Wo cong ... *lai*
I am sorry = *Duibuqi*

You can tell someone, "*Wo cong ... lai*" ("I am from ... "). If you make a mistake you might say, "*Duibuqi*" ("I am sorry").

Asking About Others

When meeting someone you might ask, *"Ni jiao shenme mingzi?"* ("What is your name?") and *"Ni shi nali ren?"* ("Where are you from?")

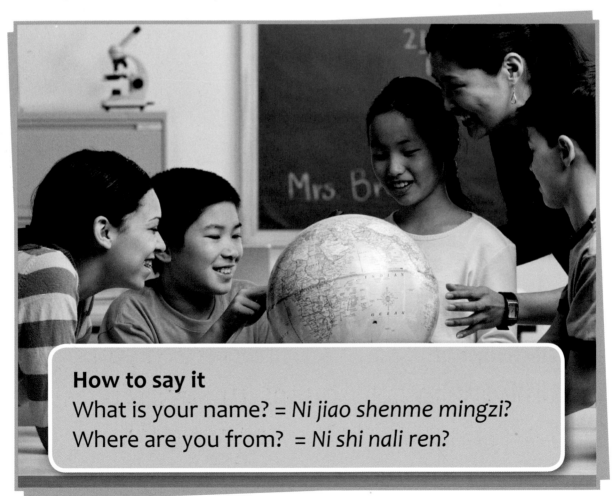

How to say it
What is your name? = *Ni jiao shenme mingzi?*
Where are you from? = *Ni shi nali ren?*

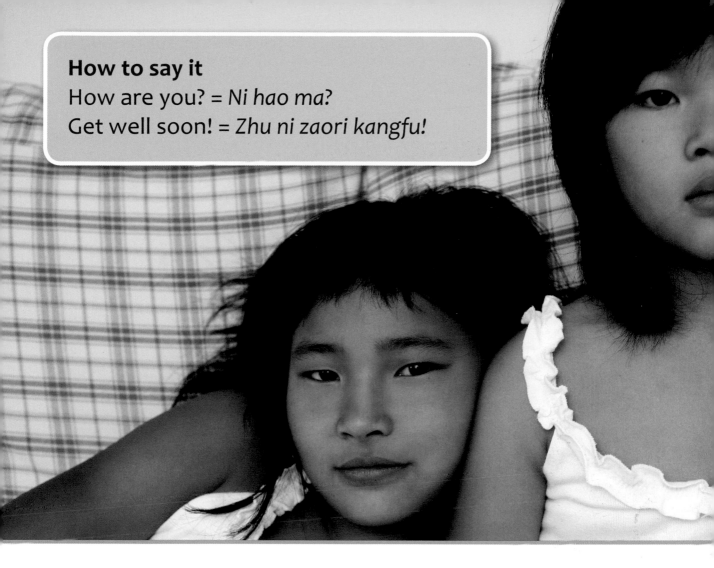

You might ask a friend or family member, "*Ni hao ma?*" ("How are you?") If someone is sick you might say, "*Zhu ni zaori kangfu!*" ("Get well soon!")

At Home

People in China may live in small villages or in big cities. They might live in tall apartment buildings, or in houses. More than 1 billion people live in China, so homes are usually small.

How to say it

village = *cunzhuang*

city = *chengshi*

house = *fangzi*

apartment building = *gongyu*

How to say it
family name = *xing*
given name = *mingzi*

In China a person's name begins with his family name, then his given name. In English we might say "Joe Smith," but in Mandarin that would be "Smith Joe." Common family names are Lee, Wang, Chen, and Zhang.

Family Life

The family is very important in China. Usually, the father goes to work. The mother may work outside the home, too.

How to say it
family = *jiating*
father = *baba*
mother = *mama*

Many Chinese families have just one child. Sometimes grandparents live with the family. So might an aunt or uncle.

At School

In China education is very important. Children have to go to school from ages 6 to 15. They go to school five days a week. Each school day begins with morning exercise.

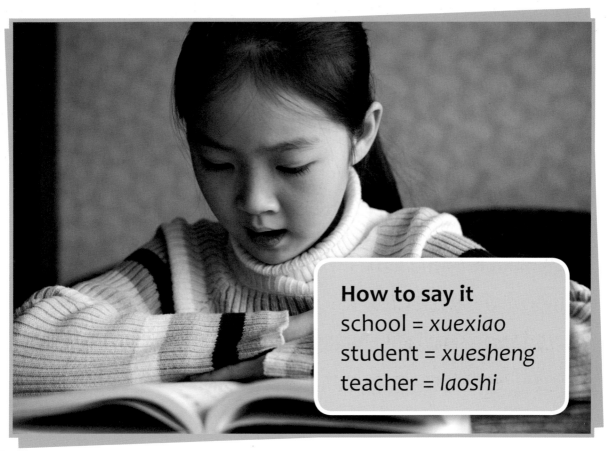

How to say it
school = *xuexiao*
student = *xuesheng*
teacher = *laoshi*

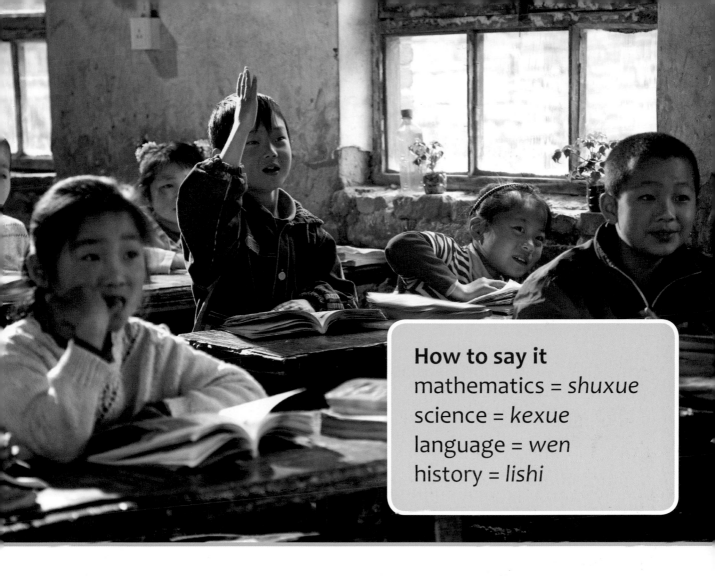

How to say it
mathematics = *shuxue*
science = *kexue*
language = *wen*
history = *lishi*

Students learn about math, history,
English, and science. All students have
to take special tests before they can go
to college or university.

Sports and Outdoors

The most popular sport in China is table tennis. Other popular sports include basketball, soccer, and golf. China held the 2008 Summer Olympic Games and won 51 gold medals.

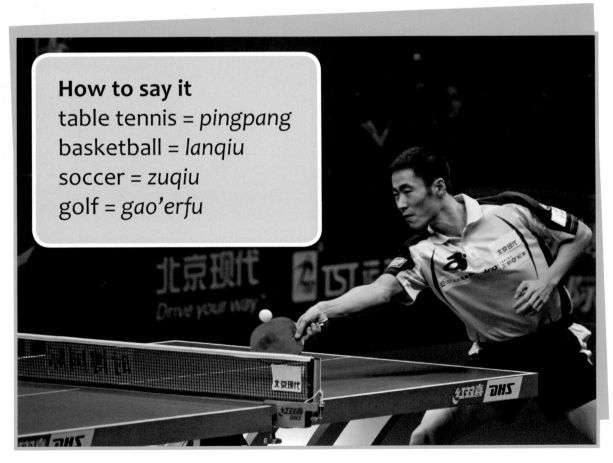

How to say it
table tennis = *pingpang*
basketball = *lanqiu*
soccer = *zuqiu*
golf = *gao'erfu*

How to say it
bicycle = *zixingche*
street = *jiedao*
crowded = *yongji*

Cities like Shanghai and Beijing are very crowded. So, many Chinese people ride bicycles to get around. They use bicycles in villages to carry supplies, too.

25

Food and Drink

Chinese food is usually simple. Main dishes include rice, noodles, fish, meat, and vegetables. Most people use chopsticks to eat. Today, there are Chinese restaurants all over the world.

How to say it
bowl = *wan*
rice = *mifan*
vegetables = *shucai*
chopsticks = *kuaizi*

How to say it
tea = *cha*
juice = *zhi*
soft drink = *yinliao*

Tea is the most popular drink in China.
People may drink it several times a day.
Juice and soft drinks are also popular.

Clothes and Shopping

Years ago Chinese men wore a suit called a *changshan*. Women wore a dress called a *qipao*. These are still worn on special occasions. Today people might wear suits to an office or jeans at home.

How to say it
suit = *xizhuang*
jeans = *niuzaiku*

Chinese people can shop at village markets or at huge shopping centers. They might buy fresh vegetables. They could buy paintings by local artists. Much of China's art shows the beauty of nature.

Pronunciation Guide

English	Mandarin	Pronunciation
apartment building	gongyu	gong you
aunt	gugu	goo goo
basketball	lanqui	lan keweeyou
bicycle	zixingche	zeezing chee
bow	jugong	jew gong
bowl	wan	wan
child	haizi	hayeezee
chopsticks	kuaizi	kooayezee
city	chengshi	cheng shee
crowded	yongji	eeyong jee
family	jiating	jeeah ting
family name	xing	zing
father	baba	baba
Get well soon!	Zhu ni zaori kangfu!	Zhoo ni zowree kangfu!
given name	mingzi	mingzee
golf	gao'erfu	gao errfoo (chueeyew)
goodbye	zaijian	zaijeear
good morning	zaochen hao	zao chen hayoh
grandparents	zufumu	zoo fuhmuh
grasshopper	mazha	maz ha
handshake	woshou	wash ohou
hello	ni hao	ne hayoh
history	lishi	lih shee
horse	ma	mah
house	fangzi	fang zee
How are you?	Ni hao ma?	Nee hayoh mah
I am from ...	Wo cong ... lai	Woah kong layee
I am sorry	Duibuqi	Dooeebuhkoowee

jeans	niuzaiku	neeooh zaaeekuw
juice	zhi	zehee
language	wen	wen/ youyan
market	shichang	sheechang
mathematics	shuxue	shoe zuuee
mother	ma / mama	ma / mama
My name is ...	Wo jiao...	Woah jeeawho
please	qing	kooing
Pleased to meet you	Hen gaoxing renshi ni	Hen gawzing renshee nee
rice	mifan	mee fan
school	xuexiao	zooeeh zeeawho
science	kexue	kerzooee
shopping center	gouwu zhongxin	gowoo zoohongzeen
smile	weixiao	wereeezeeawho
soccer	zuqiu	zoocheeow
soft drink	yinliao	yeenleeawho
street	jiedao	jeeaydaoh
student	xuesheng	zooeeesheng
suit	xizhuang	zee zoohuang
table tennis	pingpang	piing pang
tea	cha	char
teacher	laoshi	layohshee
thank you	xiexie	zeeayzeeay
traditional dress	qipao	keepaow
traditional men's suit	changshan	changshan
uncle	shushu	shooshoo
vegetables	shucai	shookay
village	cunzhuang	koonzoohooang
What is your name?	Ni jiao shenme mingzi?	Nee jeeawho shenmee mingzee
Where are you from?	Ni shi nali ren?	Nee shee narlee ren

Find Out More

Book

Roop, Peter and Connie. *A Visit to China*. Chicago: Heinemann Library, 2008.

Website

travel.nationalgeographic.com/travel/countries/ china-guide/

Index